Ripley's Believe It or Not!
Baseball Oddities & Trivia

A Journey Through the WEIRD, Wacky, and *Absolutely True* World of Baseball

by TIM O'BRIEN • • • illustrations by JOHN GRAZIANO

PLAY BALL!

Ripley Classic, 1920

Ripley's Believe It or Not! Baseball Oddities & Trivia

Copyright © 2008 by Ripley Entertainment Inc. Printed and bound in Nashville,
TN, U.S.A. All rights reserved. No part of this book may be reproduced or
transmitted in any form or by any means, electronic or mechanical, without
prior written permission from Ripley Entertainment Inc. For permission, please
contact Tim O'Brien, VP Publishing & Communications, Ripley Entertainment
Inc., 7576 Kingspointe Parkway, Suite 188, Orlando, FL, 32819; obrien@ripleys.
com. Reviewers may quote brief passages in a review to be printed in a magazine,
newspaper, or on the Web without permission from Ripley Entertainment Inc.

First printing
ISBN: 978-1-893951-29-7
Library of Congress Control Number (LCCN):

Compiled, written, and edited by: Tim O'Brien
Illustrated by: John Graziano
Cover, page, and text design by: Jennifer Wright

This book can be customized and sold in bulk for special promotional purposes.
Contact Tim O'Brien at obrien@ripleys.com for details.

For additional copies of *Ripley's Believe It or Not! Baseball Oddities & Trivia*, ask
your local bookseller to order it for you or visit www.ripleys.com, www.amazon.com,
or www.amazon.co.uk.

"This is a strange game."

-Carl Yastrzemski

Introduction

Robert Ripley wanted to play baseball nearly as much as he desired to be a successful artist. He played on sandlot teams and semi-pro teams in Santa Rosa, Calif., from 1905-1909 as a second baseman and pitcher.

He left baseball in 1909 to begin his full time artistic career as a sports illustrator in San Francisco, but he continued to dream of playing professional baseball.

In late winter 1913, he made the cross-country journey to seek fame and fortune in New York City as an illustrator. While working for the *New York Globe*, he tried out for the New York Giants in spring 1914 and made the team! The baseball card we created for our hero on the back cover of this book shows him taking a swing during spring training that year in Texas.

He broke his pitching arm during his debut game with the Giants, crushing his major league baseball dreams. It was back to the drawing boards and to the *Globe* as a full time sports illustrator, where, in 1918, he created his first Believe It or Not! cartoon based on sports, a topic he featured often through the years. Thousands of times, to be more exact.

In addition to the bevy of new facts uncovered while researching this book, I culled through more than 2,000 baseball Believe It or Not! entries currently in the Ripley archives. Many of Ripley's original baseball drawings, which I have labeled as a "Ripley Classic," are scattered throughout this book, interspersed with new illustrations by Ripley's official cartoonist of today, John Graziano.

You hold in your hands a book dedicated strictly to all things baseball. It's a journey through the weird, wacky and absolutely true world of baseball oddities and trivia.

What I have always appreciated about Ripley's Believe It or Not! is that everything presented is true and genuine! Ripley took great pride in presenting things so preposterous that their accuracy was immediately questioned. He was proven wrong only a handful of times through the years.

In keeping with the Ripley tradition, the information in this book, the first Ripley's Believe It or Not! volume dedicated specifically to baseball, is true and genuine to the best of our knowledge. Many of the sport's greatest journalists and statisticians have confirmed and reconfirmed the odd and unusual material presented here.

From a man who was stabbed to death by a baseball and a listing of some of baseball's strangest superstitions to the 2007 season when no major league team won 100 games and none lost 100 games, you'll love discovering the quirky side of baseball.

This book will reveal directly in front of you that truth is definitely more bizarre and stranger than fiction. Sit back and read it, enjoy it, but most importantly, believe it!

Tim O'Brien,
Author, VP Publishing & Communications,
Ripley Entertainment Inc.

NOVEMBER 2007

Henry Aaron, who wore uniform #44, hit 44 home runs 4 times in his career. In one of those years, he tied for the league lead with Willie McCovey, who also wore uniform #44.

St. Louis Browns infielder Buzzy Wares was left behind when the Browns finished spring training in Montgomery, Alabama in 1913. The team traded him to the minor league team that owned the stadium in exchange for the rent owed for the use of the ballpark.

On August 23, 2001, Randy Johnson of the Arizona Diamondbacks became the first Major League pitcher to strike out 300 batters in each of four consecutive seasons.

"AN EXPLOSIVE FASTBALL"

IN 1897, A PITCHING GUN USING *REAL GUNPOWDER* WAS USED BY COACHES for BATTING PRACTICE!

The Hollywood Stars of the Pacific Coast League was the first professional baseball team to fly to away games in 1928.

Toledo, Ohio's professional baseball team was known as the Mud Hens as early as 1896 and remains the only professional sports franchise in America with a feminine name.

Add Babe Ruth's year of death (1948), his age at death (53) and his uniform number (3). When totaled, it adds up to 2004, the year the Red Sox finally broke the "Curse of the Bambino."

2007
Oh What a Year!

The Mariners' Ichiro Suzuki hit the first inside-the-park home run in All-Star game history on July 10, 2007.

In 2007, no team lost 100 games; no team won 100.

On July 15, 2007, the Philadelphia Phillies became the first professional sports franchise to lose 10,000 games. The first defeat was its inaugural National League game on May 1, 1883 at the hands of the Providence R.I. Grays. Their last was on October 6, 2007 to the Colorado Rockies. The Phillies ended the 2007 season with an overall 8,853 wins; 10,028 losses.

Nice Pay Raise! Miguel Cabrera of the Florida Marlins received a salary of $7.4 million in 2007, a nice increase from the $472,000 he made in 2006!

Who's on First? In 2007, Major League first basemen averaged $3.74 million in salary, while second basemen only averaged $1.91 million.

With its 2007 victory, the New York Yankees have won 26 world championships. The St. Louis Cardinals have won the second most – 10!

IN ONE OF THE **COLDEST SPRINGS** IN THE HISTORY OF MAJOR LEAGUE BASEBALL, THE START OF THE **2007 SEASON** FOUND THAT A COLD PLAYER HITTING A COLD BASEBALL WITH A COLD BAT **PROVED TO BE DIFFICULT.** HOME RUNS AND TOTAL RUNS SCORED SANK TO THEIR LOWEST LEVEL SINCE 1993.

Major League Baseball attendance grew for the fourth consecutive season in 2007, increasing 4.5% to 79,502,524.

With a mighty swing on August 7, 2007, Barry Bonds knocked his 756th home run, making him the most prolific home run hitter in Major League Baseball annals. He ended the season with 762.

The Arizona Diamondbacks had the best record (90 wins) and the worst batting average (.250) in the National League in 2007.

As a rookie with the San Diego Padres in April 2003, Xavier Nady became the first player in Major League history whose first or last name started with an X to hit a home run. That home run went out of the field over an advertisement for radio station 91X.

The Las Vegas 51s, the Triple-A affiliate of the Los Angeles Dodgers, are named after the semi-secret government base in Nevada known as "Area 51," where UFO sightings and alien activities have allegedly taken place. Cosmo, the team's mascot from the planet Koufaxia, is (as the story goes) a survivor of a spaceship crash in Area 51.

"Statistics are to baseball what a flaky crust is to Mom's apple pie."
- Harry Reasoner

The Boston Braves' Fred Brown was a better politician than baseball player. During his two years with the Braves (1901-1902), he played in 9 games and had a .200 average. After hanging up his cleats, he was elected Democratic Governor of New Hampshire in 1923. He also served as a U.S. Senator from 1933-1939.

Warren Spahn wore #21 and won 21 games during 8 seasons.

The
PRIZE-WINNING CARTOON
of 1939

Ripley Classic, 1939

STABBED TO DEATH BY A BASEBALL!

STANTON WALKER ATTENDED A BALL GAME AND WAS SEATED BETWEEN **2** FRIENDS WHEN ONE ATTEMPTED TO PASS AN OPEN POCKET KNIFE TO THE OTHER. *JUST AS THE KNIFE PASSED IN FRONT OF WALKER IT WAS **STRUCK** BY A **FOUL BALL** AND DRIVEN INTO HIS HEART -**KILLING HIM***

MORRISTOWN -BETHESDA - MORRISTOWN, Ohio, 1902

11

BASEBALL GREAT

MARK McGWIRE
HIT 70 HOME RUNS IN 1998
THAT WENT A DISTANCE of
5.5 MILES, OR ABOUT 418.5 ft.
PER HOME RUN.
THEN HE RAN 4.8 MILES AROUND
THE BASES AFTER HITTING THEM!

American President Woodrow Wilson was the first president to attend a World Series Game and the first to throw out the first pitch. Both occurred on October 9, 1915 as the Red Sox beat the Phillies, 2 to 1.

One-armed Peter Gray, who played outfield in 77 games for the St. Louis Browns in 1945, batted .218!

In May 1951 Cleveland signed 17-year-old pitcher Billy Joe Davidson, who was being touted as the best prospect since Bob Feller, for $150,000. Three days later the Boston Red Sox signed 19-year-old infielder, Dick Pedrotti to a three-year contract for $75,000. Neither teen played a day in the Major Leagues.

Pitcher Chan Ho Park became the first player born in Korea to make the Big Leagues in the U.S. when he debuted for the Los Angeles Dodgers on April 8, 1994.

Both Major League Baseball's 1994 league MVP's, Chicago's Frank Thomas of the American League and Houston's Jeff Bagwell of the National League, were born on the same day, May 27, 1968; Frank in Columbus, Ga. and Jeff in Boston, Mass.

"Baseball is like driving, it's the one who gets home safely that counts."
– Tommy Lasorda

Three players have lead their league in batting average in a season while NOT hitting a single home run: Ginger Beaumont, National League, Pittsburgh, in 1902, with a .357 average; Zack Wheat, National League, Brooklyn in 1918, with .335; and Rod Carew, American League, Minnesota in 1972 with .318.

Between 1988 and 2005, Dr. James Andrews performed 1,128 Tommy John surgeries, more properly known as ulnar collateral ligament reconstruction (UCL). It's a surgical operation in which a ligament in the elbow is replaced with a tendon from elsewhere in the body. The procedure was developed by Dr. Frank Jobe in 1974 for pitcher Tommy John.

13

Relief pitcher Harrel Toenes of Selma, Ala., won a game against Jackson, Miss., on May 24, 1941 without throwing one pitch toward home plate. He was brought in during the top half of the 9th inning and before he threw a pitch, he picked a runner off first base, retiring the side. Selma rallied for four runs in the bottom of the ninth, winning the game and giving the victory to Toenes.

In two consecutive seasons, 1996 and 1997, Vinny Castilla of the Colorado Rockies had identical triple crown batting numbers: a .304 batting average with 40 home runs and 113 RBIs.

All Star Jitters! In 2003, Eric Gagne of the Los Angeles Dodgers won the National League Cy Young Award, but was the losing pitcher in the 2003 All-Star Game. In 2004, Roger Clemens of the Houston Astros won the Cy Young Award and was the losing pitcher in the 2004 All-Star Game.

BASEBALL BASES IN THE 1830s ORIGINALLY WERE 4-FOOT-HIGH STAKES, BUT DUE TO INJURIES TO PLAYERS THEY WERE REPLACED BY FLAT ROCKS ...

COMEDIANS **BUD ABBOTT** AND **LOU COSTELLO** ARE OFFICIAL MEMBERS OF THE BASEBALL HALL OF FAME!

San Francisco's Robby Thompson was thrown out 4 times while trying to steal bases against Cincinnati on June 27, 1986, setting a new Major League record.

Brothers Hank and Tommie Aaron hit home runs in the same game for the first time on June 12, 1962. A month later, the Milwaukee Braves teammates hit home runs in the same inning.

High school baseball standouts

and future NFL greats Dan Marino and John Elway were both chosen in the June 1979 baseball draft by the Kansas City Royals. Neither signed, opting for college. Following his sophomore year at Stanford, in 1981, Elway was drafted again, by the New York Yankees, and the following year, played 42 games for the Yankees Single-A farm club in Oneonta, New York. He hit .318, hit 4 home runs, and drove in 25 runs.

"The doctors X-rayed my head and found nothing."
- Dizzy Dean, after being hit on the head by a ball during the 1934 World Series.

In a New England League game on June 25, 1904, Lowell edged visiting Concord, 5-4. When their second baseman was ejected, Concord was left with only eight players. To avoid a forfeit, the manager put 9-year-old mascot George Diggins into the game.

Just a Kid! At 37, Sandy Koufax is the youngest inductee in the history of the Hall of Fame.

The longest game in professional baseball was played over a 3-day period in 1981 between Triple-A clubs in Pawtucket, Rhode Island and Rochester, New York. The game went 33 innings and lasted 8 hours, 25 minutes. It started April 18, a chilly Saturday evening at McCoy Stadium in Pawtucket. More than 8 hours later at 4:09 a.m. on Easter Sunday morning, April 19, the game was stopped in a 2-2 deadlock. The game was completed on June 23, with Pawtucket scoring the winning run in the bottom of the 33rd inning.

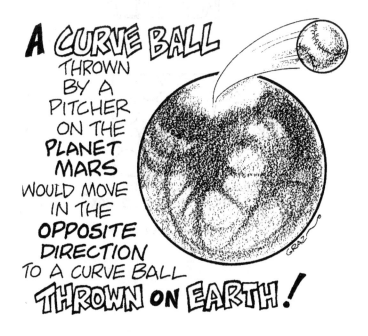

A CURVE BALL THROWN BY A PITCHER ON THE PLANET MARS WOULD MOVE IN THE OPPOSITE DIRECTION TO A CURVE BALL THROWN ON EARTH!

It wasn't until 1993 that a player in the Major Leagues hit a home run from both sides of the plate in the same inning. Carlos Baerga of the Cleveland Indians did it against the New York Yankees in the 7th inning of the April 8 game. The second Major League player, and first National League player, to accomplish it was Mark Bellhorn of the Chicago Cubs, in the 4th inning against the Milwaukee Brewers on August 29, 2002.

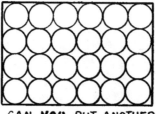

CAN **YOU** PUT ANOTHER BASEBALL IN THE ABOVE BOX?

Answer on page 52

Following a 16-year Major League career with the Senators and the Tigers, Eddie Yost became manager of the Senators, a job that lasted one game (a loss), the all-time shortest managerial career in Major League Baseball!

Why Didn't He Hit a Home Run? Lou Proctor, a Western Union telegraph operator inserted his name into the box score as a pinch hitter on May 13, 1912, for the St. Louis Browns, with no hits in one at bat. Years later, Proctor's name appeared in the first editions of The Baseball Encyclopedia but astute research in 1987 by members of the Society for American Baseball Research, un-covered the hoax and had Proctor's name purged from all official records.

Upon signing a lucrative contract Tug McGraw was asked how he planned to spend the money. "Ninety percent, I'll spend on good times, women and Irish Whiskey. The other 10% I'll probably waste."

Hall of Fame pitcher Sandy Koufax hit the first of his 2 career home runs against friend and future Hall of Fame member, Warren Spahn, on June 13, 1962.

The 2004 Kansas City Royals is the only team to ever win three straight games with identical scores while scoring in double digits – 10-4!

Matt Williams was the first Major League player to hit home runs for three different teams in World Series games: San Francisco Giants, 1989; Cleveland Indians, 1997; and the Arizona Diamondbacks, 2001.

Al Reach of the Philadelphia Athletics became the first professional salaried baseball player in 1864 – he earned $25 per week!

The 22 runs the Cleveland Indians scored in the 22-0 shellacking of the New York Yankees on August 31, 2004, are the most runs ever given up by the Yankees in their home ballpark.

The League Championships first became a 4 of 7 series in 1985.

What Movie? Film director Ben Affleck and actor Matt Damon skipped out early from the premier of their new film "Gone Baby Gone" in Boston, to watch their beloved Red Sox lose to the Indians in the 2007 ALCS game on Oct. 15.

"The Grand Old Man of Baseball," Dave Winfield of the Toronto Blue Jays, in 1992, became the first Major League player over 40 years old to bat in 100 runs in a season!

2007
It was an A-Rod Year

Alex Rodriguez won 2007's MVP

title for his impressive play for the New York Yankees, leading the league in homers, runs batted in and runs scored.

In 2007, A-Rod was the first player since

Roger Maris in 1961 to lead the majors in home runs (54), RBIs (156), AND runs (143) in one season.

"It's my third MVP and I'm here to say that I would trade all three for one world championship. I wouldn't think twice about it!" – Rodriguez, on never having been on a World Series championship team

Just teasing, I love New York!

In late October 2007, Rodriguez opted out of the last three years of his contract with the Yankees. Less than three weeks later, noting that he wanted to continue to play and set records for the Yankees, he reached a new agreement with the team that could earn him more than $300 million over the next 10-years. Under the unique agreement, A-Rod, who has 518 career homers, would receive $6 million each for tying the home run levels of Willie Mays (660), Babe Ruth (714), Hank Aaron (755) and Barry Bonds (762) He could rake in another $6 million for breaking Bond's major league homer total.

IN 1976, **MINNIE MINOSO** PLAYED FOR THE CHICAGO WHITE SOX AT THE AGE OF **53** — THE OLDEST PLAYER TO HIT IN A REGULATION GAME!

Pitcher Mitch Williams, also known as the Wild One because of his sometimes uncontrollable fast ball, was released from the Kansas City Royals in 1997 holding a dubious record. He gave up 537 hits and 544 walks in 691.1 innings pitched. He is the only Major League pitcher who pitched more than 250 innings to allow more walks than hits during his career.

"You're born with two strikes against you, so don't take a third one on your own."
– Connie Mack

The Triple-A Indianapolis Indians hit a "Homer Cycle," on May 20, 1998, a feat possibly never before duplicated in professional baseball. In the 5th inning, Pete Rose, Jr. opened the inning with a solo home run, Jason Williams connected for a 3-run shot, Glenn Murray slugged a grand slam, and Guillermo Garcia finished the scoring with a 2–run blast.

Harold Arlin, the first full time announcer on the nation's first radio station, Pittsburgh's KDKA, called the very first live broadcast of a Major League game, Pittsburgh vs. Philadelphia, on August 5, 1921.

At an average of 375 feet each, Barry Bonds' 762 home runs have traveled more than 50 miles!

Controversial player Dick Allen's younger brother Ron, is the only player to have his only hit in the Major Leagues be a home run. He hit it in 1972 during his one season of Major League ball, for the St. Louis Cardinals.

The Cure for the Curse? Boston Red Sox's Manny Ramirez fouled into Fenway Park's right field stands hitting 16-year old Lee Gavin in the face, knocking out his front two teeth. Gavin lives nearby, in a farmhouse where Babe Ruth was living when he was traded to the Yankees. Many believe that Gavin having his teeth knocked out that August 31, 2004, helped break the curse.

Padres manager Steve Boros was thrown out of a game on June 6, 1986, before the game began! He tried to give umpire Charlie Williams a videotape of a disputed play that took place during his 4–2 loss to Atlanta the night before.

Slugger Ted Williams signed with the Red Sox on Feb. 7, 1950 for $125,000, making him the then-highest paid player ever in Major League Baseball.

The Colorado Rockies, on May 5, 1999, became only the third team in modern history to score in all nine innings during their game against the Chicago Cubs.

Ripley
Classic

BABE
RUTH
WON
MORE PRIZES
**PLAYING
GOLF**
THAN HE DID
PLAYING
BASEBALL

Don't Argue with Me! On July 26, 1972, Bill Haller was the umpire behind the plate while his brother Tom was the catcher for the Detroit Tigers, a Major League first!

Spring training in Florida generates $500,000,000 for the state's economy!

ON MOTHER'S DAY IN 1939 — CLEVELAND INDIANS PITCHER **BOB FELLER** HURLED A BALL TO A CHICAGO BATTER THAT WAS FOULED OFF INTO THE STANDS AND **STRUCK HIS OWN MOTHER!**

"IT WOULD HAVE BEEN A HELLUVA LOT MORE FUN IF I HAD NOT HIT THOSE SIXTY-ONE HOME RUNS."
—ROGER MARIS

"Cliff" Heathcothe of the Chicago Cubs and Max Flack of the St. Louis Cardinals were involved in one of the most interesting trades of all times. They each played on their respective teams for the first game of a double header on May 30, 1922 and both went hitless. Team management traded them for each other between the games, and in the second game, they each played against the team they had played for only hours earlier and they each got a hit!

Night games were banned in 1943 due to wartime blackout restrictions.

As a New York Met, left-handed pitcher Al Leiter was the first pitcher in the Major Leagues to defeat all 30 teams. He accomplished the feat on April 30, 2002 when he beat the Arizona Diamondbacks 10-1.

IT TAKES A *BASEBALL* TRAVELING 89.9 MPH ONLY 400 MILLISECONDS, OR 400 ONE-THOUSANDTHS of A SINGLE SECOND, for THE BALL TO REACH *HOME PLATE!*

Radio announcer Ernie Harwell, while broadcasting for the Atlanta Crackers in 1948, caught the attention of Brooklyn Dodgers' manager Branch Rickey who traded minor league catcher Cliff Dapper to Atlanta in exchange for the broadcasting skills of Harwell.

Mary Shane became the first female TV play-by-play announcer in Major League Baseball when she was hired by the Chicago White Sox on Jan 4, 1977.

Two Milwaukee Braves rookies hit their first Major League home runs on the same day, April 23, 1954. Henry Aaron hit 754 more in his career. Charlie White hit no more.

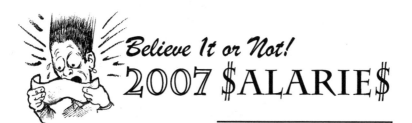

Believe It or Not!
2007 $ALARIE$

The average Major League salary of the 848 players on opening day rosters in 2007 was $2.9 million, a 5.39% increase over 2006.

The New York Yankees had an opening day roster salary of $189.6 million, more than the $185 million combined salaries of players on five other teams - Pittsburgh, Tampa Bay, Washington D.C., Florida Marlins, and Colorado.

Believe It or Not! Unlike the NBA and the NFL, Major League Baseball has no salary caps.

Three Yankees are among the top five highest paid Major League ballplayers in 2007.

Jason Giambi of the New York Yankees topped all players with a 2007 salary of $23,428,571, followed by his teammate Alex Rodriguez at $22.7 million.

IN 1966, SANDY KOUFAX SET A NATIONAL LEAGUE RECORD BY PITCHING 323 INNINGS WITHOUT HITTING A SINGLE BATTER!

GRAZIANO

President Dwight D. Eisenhower said not making the baseball team at West Point was one of the greatest disappointments in his life.

Mike Grady, an infielder for the New York Giants made 6 errors during one play in 1899! With the bases full, he dropped a batted ball, then overthrew first base, then muffed a return throw, picked it up and threw wide to the catcher, dropped the return throw and finally threw wild to 3rd base.

When Yogi Berra's wife told him she had gone to see *Dr. Zhivago* (the movie), he asked her "what's the matter with you now?"

Ray Kroc, creator of the McDonald's hamburger chain, bought the San Diego Padres in 1974 and often regretted it, once telling reporters that baseball had brought him nothing but aggravation and that there was more future in hamburgers than baseball.

Eddie Murray holds the Major League record for hitting home runs from both sides of the plate in the same game. He hit 9 while in the American League and 2 in the National League. Mickey Mantle leads the American League with 10; Ken Caminiti the National League with 10.

31

A cigar store clerk traded a box of cigars for the opportunity to pitch in a Major League game. Eddie Kolb went 8 innings for the Cleveland Spiders on October 15, 1899, for what is widely regarded as the worst Major League baseball team of all times. Kolb gave up 19 runs in the team's 134th loss of the season. The team permanently disbanded after the game.

Believe It or Not! The baseball throw was an event at the 1932 Olympic Games!

Fernando Valenzuela had a super 1981 season for the Los Angeles Dodgers – he was the first pitcher to win both the Cy Young and Rookie of the Year awards during the same season.

"MOST BALL GAMES ARE LOST, NOT WON."

— CASEY STENGEL

A BATTER CAN REACH FIRST 6 WAYS WITHOUT HITTING THE BALL

BASE ON BALLS
HIT BY PITCHED BALL
CATCHER MISSING 3RD STRIKE
SUBSTITUTE RUNNER
CATCHER INTERFERENCE
CATCHER TIPPING BAT

Joel Youngblood became the first Major League player to get base hits for two different teams in two different cities on the same day. As a New York Met, he singled during an afternoon game in Chicago on August 4, 1982, and was informed immediately after that game that he had been traded to Montreal. He flew to Philadelphia, caught up with his new team, was put into right field and got a base hit that evening.

Ty Cobb walked up to 30 miles
a day during the off-season with lead in his shoes to maintain his lower body strength.

A HALF INNING IS ONE INNING!

AN *"INNING"* IS THE TERM AT BAT
OF **9** PLAYERS REPRESENTING
A CLUB IN A GAME AND IS
COMPLETED WHEN **3** OF SUCH
PLAYERS HAVE BEEN LEGALLY
PUT OUT

RULE 69-SEC.4
OFFICIAL BASE BALL RULES

Sam Chapman of the Philadelphia Athletics, hit
2 home runs in 2 days in the same game against the
Chicago White Sox, July 30-31, 1941. During the
night game, he hit one homer before midnight and
one homer after midnight!

Eighteen-year-old Bob Feller requested a
short leave from the Cleveland Indians in May 1937
to attend his high school graduation. After insuring
him for $100,000, team management allowed him to
fly home.

In 2001, when Barry Bonds shattered Babe Ruth's home run record with 73 homers, he also bested Ruth's best slugging percentage with a .863 and Ruth's record of base-on-balls by walking 177 times.

Tony Perez had the exact same number of 2Bs, 3B,s, HRs, and RBIs; 32-6-19-91 in two consecutive seasons, 1976 for the Cincinnati Red and 1977 for the Montreal Expos.

More than Socks!

The Chicago White Sox changed their uniform styles 57 times between 1901 and the early 1990s.

"Baseball players are smarter than football players. How often do you see a baseball team penalized for too many men on the field?"
— Jim Bouton

The Chicago Cubs' Andre Dawson won the MVP Award on November 18, 1987, the first time a player from a last place team earned that honor.

Before they won it in 2004, the Boston Red Sox's previous World Series championship took place in 1918. Game 1 of that World Series lasted 1 hour, 50 minutes. In 2004, Game 1 lasted 4 hours, 0 minutes.

A New Era for Baseball in our Nation's Capital

A sellout crowd of 45,596 fans came out to see the premier of the new Washington Nationals at RFK Stadium in Washington DC on April 14, 2005. The game marked the return of Major League Baseball to the Nation's Capital after a 34-year absence.

When President George W. Bush

threw out the first pitch for the Washington Nationals' first game on April 14, 2005, he became the 12th U.S. President to throw out the first pitch for a Washington DC Major League Baseball team.

The ball that President George W.

Bush threw across the plate on April 14, 2005 for the Washington Nationals was the same ball used by pitcher Joe Grzenda to throw the last pitch for the old Washington Senators on September 30, 1971.

As a player, Frank Robinson, manager of the Nationals, played in 2,808 games, including 12 All-Star games and 26 World Series games. Prior to the Nationals' his record as a manager was 591 wins, 642 losses.

Ripley Classic

PRESIDENT WILLIAM HOWARD TAFT
IN 1910, IN A BASEBALL GAME BETWEEN
THE WASHINGTON SENATORS AND
PHILADELPHIA ATHLETICS, **STARTED
THE PRESIDENTIAL CUSTOM OF**
THROWING OUT THE FIRST BALL

Believe It or Not! Hall of Fame pitcher "Old Hoss" Radbourne finished all his 73 starts for Providence during the regular season and then went on to help his team win the World Series by pitching every inning. He ended the 1884 season with 60 wins, 441 strike outs, and a 1.38 ERA. During the season he won 18 consecutive games and pitched 11 shutouts.

Ripley Classic

"BABE RUTH" OF THE AZTECS
BRONZE FIGURE
CENTURIES OLD FOUND IN MICHOACÁN, Mexico

IT IS POSSIBLE TO PLAY 9 INNINGS ON 9 PITCHED BALLS

FIRST BATTER TRIPLES ON FIRST PITCHED BALL ——— THEN TRIES TO STEAL HOME. PITCHER STEPS FROM BOX AND THROWS HOME BATTER INTERFERES WITH THROW. THEREFORE BATTER IS OUT, AND RUNNER GOES BACK TO THIRD. THE NEXT TWO BATTERS GO OUT THE SAME WAY. THIS IS REPEATED FOR THE ENTIRE NINE INNINGS

In one game on April 22, 1928, Stanley Hawkins, a center fielder from Mountain View, California, got 4 hits in 4 times at bat, stole 4 bases, scored 4 times, and caught 4 fly balls. During that season he played in 44 games and batted .444 for the year.

Joe McCarthy, the manager who led the New York Yankees to 8 American League pennants, spent 20 seasons as a player and manager in the minor leagues, but never played a single inning in the big league.

Chasing down a fly ball in Yankee Stadium, Cleveland Indians' Larry Brown and Leon Wagner were injured in one of the most serious collisions in Major League history. Wagner broke his nose and received a slight concussion. Brown suffered fractures of the skull, nose and cheek!

Brooks Kieschnick of the Milwaukee Brewers was the first Major League player to hit a home run as a pitcher, a designated hitter and a pinch hitter - all in the same season!

Chicago Cubs switch-hitter Augie Galan became the first National League player to hit homers from both sides of the plate in the same game on June 25, 1937.

Jeremy Giambi hit 8 home runs in each league BEFORE the All-Star break in 2002, the first to ever do so in the Major Leagues. He started the season with the Oakland Athletics and was traded to the Philadelphia Phillies.

Big Hits in Cincinnati. Three 500-home run hitters appeared in the same game for the first time on June 10, 2005 when the Reds (Ken Griffey Jr.) hosted the Orioles (Sammy Sosa and Rafael Palmeiro).

UMPIRES ONCE INVITED CRITICISM. **BASEBALL UMPIRES** IN THE 1800s WORE TOP HATS AND ASKED BOTH PLAYERS AND SPECTATORS FOR THEIR OPINIONS ON QUESTIONABLE CALLS!

41

Hall of Fame basketball star Bill Sharman is
the only man in Major League Baseball history to
be thrown out of a game without ever having played
in one. On September 27, 1951, having been called
up by the Brooklyn Dodgers from the minors late in
the season, Sharman was sitting on the bench when
a shouting match over a disputed play took place
between the plate umpire and the Dodgers' bench.
In retaliation, the umpire ejected the entire team,
including Sharman from the game!

The Pittsburgh Pirates beat the Baltimore Orioles
4-3 in the first World Series game to be played at night,
October 13, 1971.

"THE LONGEST HOME RUN"
BABE RUTH, DURING AN EXHIBITION
GAME, HIT A BALL THAT LANDED
ON A MOVING TRAIN THAT
CARRIED IT FOR OVER
200 MILES!

Lucky 7's

No. 7 Cesar Gutierrez of the Tigers accomplished the rare feat of 7 hits in 7 at bat on June 12, 1970. The following year, he only had 7 hits during the entire season.

Charlie Kerfeld wore #37 for the Houston Astros and was so fond of the number that he requested that his salary for the 1987 season be $110,037.37!

Effa Manley, general manager and co-owner of the Newark Eagles team of the Negro Leagues, became the first female member of the Baseball Hall of Fame in 2006!

The shortest 9-inning Major League baseball game took place on Sept. 28, 1919 when the N.Y. Giants defeated the Philadelphia Phillies, 6-1 in 51 minutes.

Following graduation from Umpire School in 1969, Bernice Gera fought in the courts for 3 years to gain the right to work in the New York-Penn League. She beat the courts in 1972 and her first assignment was a double-header featuring Auburn and Geneva. During the first game an argument over a controversial call left her in tears. She resigned after that one game and never umpired for professional baseball again!

Ila Borders of the Duluth-Superior Dukes became the first female pitcher to start a Minor League game. She was credited with two strikeouts but gave up 5 hits and 2 walks in her team's 8-3 loss to the Sioux Falls Canaries in the Northern League.

"Anybody who's ever had the privilege of seeing me play knows that I am the greatest pitcher in the world."
– Dizzy Dean

Belt Loops did not become standard on men's trousers until after WW I, but baseball players were using them on their knickers as early as the 1800s!

The Angels' Fred Lynn hit the first grand slam homerun in an All-Star game on July 6, 1983.

During one game between the Chicago Cubs and the Boston Braves, 78 foul balls were hit into the grandstand.

BABE RUTH HIT HIS FIRST PROFESSIONAL HOME RUN in Canada AND HIS LAST PROFESSIONAL HOME RUN in Mexico!

During the second game of the 1945 World Series

between the St. Louis Browns and the St. Louis Cardinals, the Browns committed six errors on one play. Emil Verban of the Cardinals hit a single and Max Lanier popped up a bunt between the pitcher and the foul line. Nelson Potter and Mark Christman ran after the ball, looked at each other, and let it drop between them. Potter grabbed the ball and bobbled it. That's two. He picked it up, threw wild to first. That's three. Don Gutteridge was covering first and instead of going after the wild throw, he kept his foot on the bag and missed the throw. That's four. The ball rolled into the corner, hit the fence and bounced back and went between the legs of Chet Laabs. That's five. Laabs picked up the ball, and threw wild to second. The ball rolled into the outfield. That's six. The Cardinals won.

A BASEBALL PLAYER TO HIT A HOME RUN, MUST STRIKE THE BALL WITH A FORCE EQUIVALENT TO 1,400 POUNDS -- HE'LL MISS IF HE SWINGS 3 MILLISECONDS TOO EARLY OR TOO LATE

New York Yankees' pitcher David Wells pitched the first inning of a game against Cleveland on June 28, 1997 wearing a cap autographed by Babe Ruth. He pitched a shutout inning, but Manager Joe Torre made him take off the cap before returning to the mound in the second inning, Wells blew a 3-0 lead in the second inning wearing his own cap.

Baseball great George Brett is the only player to win batting titles in 3 different decades, hitting .333 in 1976; .390 in 1980; and .329 in 1990!

A semi-pro baseball game in Gallup, New Mexico, on July 4, 1933 was called during the afternoon because of hot weather. Two hours later when it cooled down, the game was called again - because of a snowstorm!

BASEBALL
HALL OF FAME
PITCHER **HOYT WILHELM**
HIT THE ONLY HOME RUN OF HIS
20-YEAR MAJOR LEAGUE CAREER
THE FIRST TIME HE STEPPED UP TO THE
PLATE ON APRIL 23, 1952 FOR THE
NEW YORK GIANTS.

Ray Chapman, the Cleveland shortstop who was killed by a pitched ball on August 16, 1920, had the following record in the box score for that game: "AB2/R2/H2/PO2/SB2/A2/E2/ and he was twice hit by a pitched ball." No mention of his death.

TAKE ME OUT TO THE... OPERA?!!
"THE MIGHTY CASEY,"
THE ONLY OPERA **EVER** WRITTEN ABOUT BASEBALL, WAS COMPOSED BY AMERICAN WILLIAM SCHUMAN AND PREMIERED IN HARTFORD, CONN. IN 1953!

Gaylord Perry became the first pitcher to win a Cy Young Award from each league on October 25, 1978.

> **"The trouble with baseball is that it is not played the year round."**
> – Gaylord Perry

Ken Griffey Jr. and Sr.

became the first father and son to play on the same team at the same time when Sr. joined the Seattle Mariners for one season, a team his son had joined the year before.

Enrique Oliu delivers Spanish broadcasts of home games by the Tampa Bay Devil Rays Baseball Team - yet he has been blind since birth.

Smallest strike zone ever!

Eddie Gaedel, a midget showman who stood 3 feet, 7-inches tall and weighed only 65-pounds made an official appearance as a pinch hitter for the St. Louis Browns in a game against the Detroit Tigers on August 19, 1951. The number on the back of his uniform was 1/8. In his batting stance, his strike zone measured only 1 1/2 inches! He walked on four straight pitches in his only game appearance. Gaedel's appearance was a stunt created by Bill Veeck, the Browns' owner, who paid him $100.

A pitcher can win a complete 9-inning game without throwing a ball or a strike, or winning the game by forfeit. How? First batter up waits until the pitcher is ready to pitch, then crosses over to the other side of the batter's box. All batters do likewise and all are declared out without a ball being thrown! Rule 44, Sec. 10 of the official baseball rules.

In 1922, as a 15-year old, William Bendix, who later became a famous actor with two-dozen TV shows and movies to his credit, was a batboy for the New York Yankees, and made pre-game trips to the concession stands to gather snacks for Babe Ruth. One day, following a huge pre-game munch-out, Ruth collapsed and was rushed to the hospital with stomach pains. He was diagnosed with severe indigestion, but the front office fired Bendix, faulting him for bringing the Babe too much food. Bendix 26 years later, starred as the Babe in the box office flop, *The Babe Ruth Story*.

"Don't worry, the fans don't start booing until July."
– Earl Weaver

Dick Fowler of the Philadelphia Athletics, left the team in 1942 for a stint in the Canadian Army. Upon his return in 1945, he pitched a no-hit, no-run game in his first appearance!

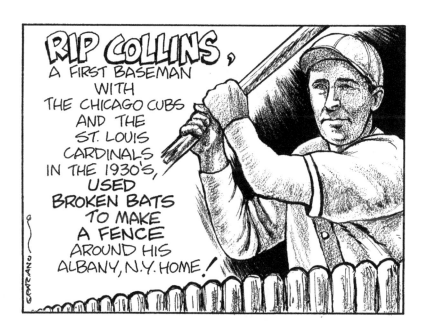

Boston Red Sox's Scott Hatteberg was the first player in Major League history to hit into a triple play and hit a grand slam during the same game, on August 6, 2001.

Leaving Major League baseball after playing in 912 games in 13 seasons, John Berardino, dropped the final "r" from his name and starred as Dr. Steve Hardy for more than 25 years on TV's *General Hospital*.

51

RIPLEY's RIDDLE

Answer from page 18:

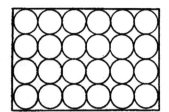

BOX CONTAINING **24** BASEBALLS

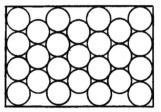

THE **SAME BOX** CONTAINING **25** BALLS

" THE WAY TO MAKE COACHES THINK YOU'RE IN SHAPE IN THE SPRING IS TO GET A TAN. "

— WHITEY FORD

Rich Tiberi of Kentucky purchased a box of unidentified baseballs for $250 from a collectibles store. The box contained balls autographed by Babe Ruth, Tony Lazzeri and Lou Gehrig: valued at about $20,000!

All 9 Cleveland players had a hit and scored a run in the 5th inning of a game against Boston on June 8, 1908.

"Casey at the Bat," the baseball poem written by Ernest Lawrence Thayer has been popular for more than a century, yet Thayer wrote it in only 2 hours and was paid only $5 for it. He was so embarrassed by his creation that he did not admit to writing it for years!

In 2001, the Milwaukee Brewers became the first Major League team to end a season with more strikeouts (1,399) than hits (1,378).

Bert Shepard, a pitcher for the Washington Senators in 1946, had a wooden leg!

Barry Bond's slugging ability has been so feared that he has been intentionally walked more than anyone else in baseball history – 686 times! He also leads MLB with the most walks in a career – 2,558!

A baseball hit 400 feet is subject to twice as much destructive energy as a bullet fired from a .8 caliber pistol.

UMPIRE **BOB EMSLIE** (1859-1943)
USED HOTEL REGISTRY BOOKS
TUCKED UNDER HIS SHIRT FOR
PROTECTION FROM STRAY BALLS!

SUPERSTITIONS

Long-standing: If a player sees a cross-eyed woman in the grandstand he will not get a hit during the game.

Jackie Robinson never stepped into the batter's box until the catcher was in position, then he walked in front of him rather than behind.

Babe Ruth would never let a teammate use one of his bats. He believed each bat had only so many hits in it and he didn't want someone taking away his hits.

Willie Mays always kicked second base on the way back to the dugout from centerfield.

Carl Hubbell never stepped on foul lines.

No reason for superstition. On Friday, June 13, 1975, #13 Dave Concepcion stole his 13th base of the season against the Cubs at Wrigley Field.

Rochester clinched an International League pennant on Friday the 13th, beating Buffalo in their 13th match of the season by a score of 13-0.

By executive decree in 1978, the No. 13 was banned from uniforms throughout the Atlanta Braves system.

From the late 1800s: It is good luck to pass a wagon loaded with hay on your way to the ballpark.

In 1949, during an amateur baseball game in Florida, a lightning bolt killed the first baseman, second baseman and the short stop, and injured 30 spectators while cutting a 20-foot ditch across the infield!

President Ronald Reagan kidding with Gaylord Perry:

"I just know its an ugly rumor that you and I are the only two people left alive who saw Abner Doubleday throw out the first pitch."

Sandy Koufax was the first pitcher in Major League history to throw 4 no-hitters during a career. His 4th no hitter was a perfect game, on September 9, 1965.

Mario Cuomo, former governor of New York State, signed with the Pittsburgh Pirates in 1951 and played the following year for the Class D Brunswick (Georgia) Pirates. He played in 81 games, hitting .244 before he was beaned by a pitched ball and spent two weeks in the hospital. Upon his hospital release, Cuomo retired from baseball and entered law school.

The Detroit Tigers and the Oakland A's set an American League record for most hurlers used in an 18-inning double-header (21) on July 23, 1961.

The words "strike" and "hit" are synonymous in meaning unless used in baseball parlance.

Ripley
Classic,
1935

DICK
BARTELL
Giants'
Shortstop
IN THE
FIRST INNING
OF THE
FIRST GAME
DURING THE
FIRST WEEK-
HIT THE
FIRST BALL
FOR HIS
FIRST HOME RUN
IN HIS
FIRST HOME GAME   1935

Ripley Classic

AL GREEN of New York City RETRIEVED 211 BASEBALLS HIT INTO THE GRANDSTAND IN 4 YEARS!

The first World Series game played on foreign soil
was between the Toronto Blue Jays and Atlanta Braves
on October 20, 1992 at the Sky Dome (now Rogers
Centre) in Toronto.

Eddie Rose, during a semi-pro game in New
Orleans killed a pigeon with a batted ball during a
game. He was credited with a hit!

Pittsburgh's Eddie O'Brien and Johnny O'Brien
were the first twins to play for the same team in the
same game, on May 10, 1953.

For the first time since 1904, the World Series was
called off in 1994, due to the player's strike that lasted
into the 1995 season for a total of 234 days.

The Cleveland, Ohio Library maintains the world's
largest collection of baseball printed memorabilia.

Wally Gerber of the St. Louis Browns batted twice
in succession in 1927. He batted out of turn and
nobody noticed!

In 1944, Joe Nuxhall joined the Cincinnati Reds as
a pitcher at the age of 15! He went on to pitch 2,303
innings and win 135 games during his career.

If a baseball game were played on the moon, an average Major League home run would travel 4,200 feet!

Hall of Fame pitcher Dizzy Dean became a sports announcer following his Major League career and was soon criticized by school teachers for his bad grammar. His response to them: "There are a lot of school teachers who ain't using ain't, but they ain't eating."

Bob Feller, the Cleveland Indians celebrated pitcher, discovered he had a Major League fastball at the age of 12 when one of his pitches broke three of his father's ribs.

THE PHILADELPHIA ATHLETICS
IN WINNING A BASEBALL DOUBLE-HEADER ON OCT. 20, 1865, SCORED 261 RUNS IN ONE DAY

"Pesapallo," the national sport of Finland, is derived from baseball but first base is at third, the pitcher tosses the ball straight up in the air, and hitting the ball out of the park is a foul!

Thinking Positive! Ty Cobb was challenged by a fan in 1916 who claimed he could strike Cobb out on three pitches. When Cobb proceeded to hit three home runs in a row, the fan said: "I don't believe that's Ty Cobb!"

"It took me 17 years to get 3,000 hits in baseball. I did it in one afternoon on the golf course."
– Hank Aaron

MLB.com presented the first Major League game to be streamed live on broadband Internet on August 26, 2002 between the Texas Rangers and the New York Yankees.

The Best and the Worst! Pitcher Phil Niekro of the Atlanta Braves led the National League in 1979 for most games won, 21; and most games lost, 20.

Montreal Expos pitcher Bill Lee, known for his candid comments and actions, once asked Expos management if he could wear #337 on his jersey. That way, he explained, the fans could read his name if he stood on his head.

Believe It or Not! The old Chicago White Sox, under the direction of Cap Anson, were a classy bunch. In the 1880s, they showed up in formal evening dress and played a regulation game dressed to the nines.

The Chicago Cubs defeated the New York Mets, 5-3 on March 29, 2000 at the Tokyo Dome in the first Major League game ever played on Asian soil.

Roberto Clemente was the first Hispanic player to be enshrined into the Baseball Hall of Fame, on July 6, 1973.

"I made a game effort to argue but two things were against me: the umpires and the rules."
– Leo Durocher

Greg Harris was an ambidextrous hurler who was never permitted to throw from both sides of the mound in the same game during his career. That is until his last game before retirement! On September 28, 1995, while pitching with the Montreal Expos against the Cincinnati Reds, in the 9th inning, he became the only 20th century pitcher to throw from both sides of the mound in the same game. The six fingered, ambidextrous glove Harris wore is now in the Baseball Hall of Fame.

President George W. Bush is the only Little League player to become President of the United States.

Why did TURK WENDELL, a pitcher who played for the Chicago Cubs, New York Mets, Philadelphia Phillies and the Colorado Rockies (1993-2004) *brush his teeth between every inning?*

Answer on page 86

The longest distance a single baseball has ever traveled is 6,600,000 miles. It was carried into orbit aboard the space shuttle Columbia in 1995!

Grand Debut! Houston Astros outfielder, 18-year old John Paciorek, in his one and only Major League appearance, went 3 for 3 at the plate, walked twice, drove in 3 runs and scored 4 times, during the team's last game of the season on September 29, 1963.

Mike Carmichael of Alexandria Ind., has applied a coat of paint to a regulation baseball every day since 1977. Believe It or Not! the ball is now covered with more than 18,000 coats of paint and weighs 1,300 pounds!

Jackie Robinson

Black Heritage usa 20c

JACKIE ROBINSON
OF THE OLD BROOKLYN DODGERS,
WHO BROKE THE COLOR BARRIER
IN BIG LEAGUE BASEBALL, WAS
IN 1982 THE FIRST INDIVIDUAL
BALL PLAYER TO BE COMMEMORATED
ON A U.S. POSTAGE STAMP.

The earliest Opening Day in Major League Baseball took place on March 30, 2004 when the Tampa Bay Devil Rays beat the New York Yankees, 8-3 before a crowd of 55,000 in the Tokyo (Japan) Dome.

"I would rather beat the Yankees regularly than pitch a no hit game."
– Bob Feller

Only three players have stolen at least one base in each of four different decades: Ted Williams, Rickey Henderson, and Tim Raines Sr.

Major League pitcher Calvin Coolidge Julius Caesar Tuskahoma McLish, shortened to Cal, was the only child of eight who his father was permitted to name. His friends called him Buster during his professional career, 1944-1964.

Jess Dobernick of the Los Angeles Angels faced only 27 men, allowed no hits, no runs, yet his team lost 3-0. How did that happen? He relieved another pitcher in the first inning with no outs after 3 runs had already scored.

Tommy Lasorda's Major League pitching premiere for the Brooklyn Dodgers lasted only one inning on May 5, 1955. During that one inning, he matched a National League record – by throwing 3 wild pitches!

Realizing that moisture on a baseball causes it to drop dramatically, Bobby Mathews, who later pitched a 297-248 won/loss record in the Major Leagues, is credited for inventing the spitball in 1868.

Believe it or Not! A homerun was hit in every inning of the July 10, 1929 contest between Pittsburgh and Philadelphia. The Phillies hit 4 and the Pirates hit 5 during its 15-9 victory.

BOB WALK
the Atlanta Braves'
pitcher **WALKED**
Duane **WALKER,**
outfielder
for the Cincinnati Reds
(July 4, 1982)

Slugger Pete Browning, during one of his batting slumps in 1884, had a bat custom made for him in a wood shop in Louisville, KY. With that bat, he immediately pulled out of his slump and the little shop, Hillerich & Bradsby, started creating bats for others, becoming famous for a line of bats it named after Browning – the Louisville Slugger.

Walter Alston, successful in the minor leagues as a player and then as a manager, struck out his only time at bat in the Major Leagues during the one game he played for the St. Louis Cardinals in 1936.

Lou Gehrig played the 1934 season with a broken toe to keep from breaking his successive games record.

The size of the baseball
diamond has not changed since
Alexander Cartwright stepped
off 90-feet between bases
165 years ago!

The most evenly matched game in the history of
Major League Baseball took place on August 13, 1910.
The Brooklyn Dodgers were playing at home against the
Pittsburgh Pirates. The game was tied after 9-innings
when it was called due to darkness. The scores weren't
the only identical stats in this game. Each team had
13 hits in 38 at bat; 27 putouts; 12 assists and 2 errors.
Each team used 10 players, including 2 pitchers who
each recorded 3 walks, 5 strikeouts and each hit a batter.
Both second basemen had 2 hits and scored 2 runs; and
each catcher had a passed ball, 6 putouts, batted 4 times
and had 1 hit. Both short stops had 2 hits; both first
basemen scored 1 run; each right fielder had 2 hits in 5
at bat and each had a putout. Both center fielders had 2
putouts and batted 5 times.

Mickey Mantle smacked the first home run ever hit in a domed stadium during the first game played in the Houston Astrodome on April 9, 1965.

Carl Yastrzemski, who in 1961 replaced Ted Williams in left field, played all his 3,308 Major League games, over a 23-year period, as a Boston Red Sox.

Chicago Cubs owner Bill Veeck hired midgets as vendors for opening day 1961, thinking they wouldn't block the view of the field as much as regular size vendors. The trays proved to be too large and heavy for the midgets to carry and they spilled beer, soda and peanuts all over the stadium.

The first umpire to use video playback to reverse a play was Frank Pulli. His reversal on May 31, 1999 took away a Marlins' home run against the Cardinals.

The Yankees' Les Nunamaker was the only catcher in the 20th century to throw out three players trying to steal bases in the same inning.

Cuban dictator Fidel Castro was a college all-star baseball player for the University of Havana. In 1949, the New York Giants were so impressed they offered him the standard $5,000 signing bonus. Several days later, he declined the offer noting that he wanted to help people for a living and keep baseball as a hobby.

Ripley Classic

ROY ACUFF

THE TENNESSEAN CALLED THE
FATHER OF COUNTRY MUSIC,
HAD PLANNED TO BE A
PROFESSIONAL BASEBALL
PLAYER--*BUT HIS BALL
CAREER ENDED ABRUPTLY
DURING SUMMER TRAINING
WITH THE YANKEES WHEN HE
SUFFERED A SUNSTROKE*

71

Ripley Classic

High Balls

ROBERT
"PHIL"
BAKER
captain
of the old
Washington, D.C.
baseball
team

CAUGHT
A BALL
THROWN
FROM THE
TOP OF THE
WASHINGTON
MONUMENT
IN ONE
BARE
HAND

*THE
IMPACT
BROKE
2
KNUCKLES*

On March 13, 1915, Brooklyn manager Wilbert Robinson was set to catch a baseball dropped from a plane flying at 525 feet. Pilot Ruth Law "forgot" to take a baseball and dropped a grapefruit instead, which splattered all over Robinson as he attempted to catch it. Casey Stengel, then outfielder for the team, was blamed for the switch.

Joe Sprinz of the San Francisco Seals of the Pacific Coast League, tried to break the altitude record for a catch in a stunt during the Treasure Island Exhibition in August 1939. The ball was dropped 800 feet from a blimp and hit him in the face. He suffered a compound fracture of the jaw and the loss of several teeth.

Babe Ruth caught a baseball dropped from an airplane 250 feet above Mitchell Field in New York on July 22, 1926.

"BASEBALL IS 90 % MENTAL. THE OTHER HALF IS PHYSICAL."
—YOGI BERRA

Contrary to popular belief, the game of baseball was not invented, it evolved through the years to what it is today. From the first recorded game in 1845, through the first professional teams of the 1860s into the 1870s and 1880s, the later half of the 19th century was baseball's most formative period from which the basic rules of today were gradually evolved.

Dixie Walker hit a home run and caught the ball himself! It happened in Ebbets Field in 1948. The ball remained lodged in the right field screen until after the game when Walker shook the ball loose and caught it!

The Toronto Blue Jays became the first team from Canada to win the World Series when they defeated the Atlanta Braves 4 games to 2 in the 1992 series.

Charley Gelbert, the St. Louis Cardinals hero of the 1930 World Series, played 239 Major League games in 1935 on a leg that had nearly been severed two years earlier. He was accidentally shot while hunting in 1932 and his fibula was entirely disconnected and four inches of the posterior artery and nerve were completely destroyed. After two years, most of which were spent on crutches, he signed with his old club. He played for another five years.

Arizona Diamondbacks' Randy Johnson became the first left-handed pitcher to strike out 20 batters during a single game on May 8, 2001.

The 2004 Rookie of the Year Award went to Jason Bay of the Pittsburgh Pirates, the first Canadian-born recipient of the trophy.

Hall of Fame infielder Rogers Hornsby, considered one of the greatest right-handed batters of all times, never went to the movies or read a book, in fear they would impair his vision.

THE **ONLY TRIPLE HALL OF FAMER** **CAL HUBBARD** of Keytesville, Mo., WAS ELECTED TO *THE COLLEGE FOOTBALL HALL OF FAME, THE NATIONAL FOOTBALL LEAGUE'S HALL OF FAME AND THE PROFESSIONAL BASEBALL HALL OF FAME*

IN 1919, RAY "SLIM" CALDWELL, A PITCHER FOR THE CLEVELAND INDIANS, WAS STRUCK BY LIGHTNING DURING A GAME *BUT WAS REVIVED AND CONTINUED TO PLAY!*

Believe it or Not! The Alijadoes Baseball Park in Tampico, Mexico, built in 1927, had a railroad track through the middle of the infield, forcing players to stop the game whenever a train passed by!

Throughout history, 60 pitchers surrendered a home run to the first batter they faced in the Major Leagues. Five of them got tagged on their first-ever PITCH!

On October 5, 1921, KDKA, with Grantland Rice, the New York sports writer calling the plays, broadcast the first World Series game ever heard on radio. Only the first game between the New York Yankees and the New York Giants was broadcast that year.

Babe Ruth could throw two baseballs at the same time with both balls staying parallel to each other from the pitcher's mound to the catcher's mitt!

Washington Senators' Walter Johnson, while pitching on April 15, 1911, struck out 4 batters in one inning! One man reached first base when the catcher dropped the ball on the third strike.

Vean Gregg struck out 367 men in 395 innings for the Pacific Coast League during the 1910 season.

"Hello again, everybody. It's a bee-yooo-tiful day for baseball."
– Harry Caray

During the August 22, 2007, 30–3 trouncing of the Baltimore Orioles, the Texas Rangers became the first Major League Baseball team since 1897 to score 30 runs in a game. During the second half of that double-header, the Rangers scored an additional 9 runs in their win, setting the record for most runs scored by an American League team in one day!

The Cincinnati Red Stockings, the first professional baseball team, traveled 11,877 miles to play games in 1869 and ended the season with a profit of $1.39.

Happy Birthday Homers: As a shortstop with the Boston Red Sox, Nomar Garciaparra is the only Major League player to hit 3 home runs on his birthday, July 23, 2002.

"Going to bed with a woman never hurt a ball player. It's staying up all night looking for them that does you in."
– Casey Stengel

In 1945, Detroit Tigers pitcher Virgil Trucks became the only pitcher to ever win a World Series game without winning a single game during the regular season!

During a Yankees game in the 1930s, Lyn Lary was on first with two out. Lou Gehrig hit a home run over the fence but nobody scored! Lary thought the ball was caught and ran to the dugout. Gehrig was declared out for passing a runner.

In 1965, during the Major League All-Star Game, Hall of Famer Willie Stargell hit a home run that landed inside the tuba of a marching band member.

Lynn Myers, playing in Asheville, N.C., scored 7 runs in one game without being officially at bat! He walked 5 times and was twice hit by a pitch. He scored all seven times he got on base.

St. Louis Browns owner Bill Veeck created many of today's successful gate promotions, including Bat Day, Ball Day and Jacket Day. It all started in 1951 when Veeck bought 6,000 bats at a big discount from a company that was going bankrupt. He offered them free to each youngster attending the game accompanied by an adult.

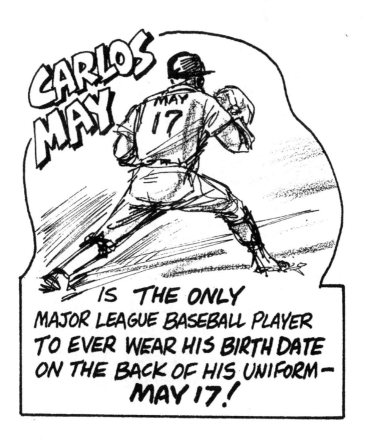

CARLOS MAY IS THE ONLY MAJOR LEAGUE BASEBALL PLAYER TO EVER WEAR HIS BIRTH DATE ON THE BACK OF HIS UNIFORM — MAY 17!

The First Baseball Fine

A PLAYER IN THE WORLD'S FIRST BASEBALL GAME PLAYED IN HOBOKEN, N.J., ON JUNE 19, 1846, WAS FINED 6 CENTS BY UMPIRE ALEXANDER CARTWRIGHT FOR SWEARING!

The highest scoring professional game on record took place on June 8, 1869 when two Buffalo, New York teams hammered it out in a three-hour game. The Niagaras beat the Colombias, 209-10. Niagra scored 58 runs in the 8th inning.

Ed Linke of the Washington Senators was pitching against the Yankees on July 26, 1935 when a line drive from a batter struck him in the head. The ball rebounded back to catcher Jack Redmond on the fly who caught it and then threw the runner out at second base for a double play. Linke was knocked out, but was given an assist on the play, while unconscious. He was hospitalized for three days, but came back to pitch 8 victories in a row.

"The day I got a hit off Sandy Koufax was when he knew it was all over."
– Sparky Anderson

After playing in a record 2,632 consecutive games, Cal Ripken Jr. pulled himself out of the Orioles lineup prior to the game on September 20, 1998, breaking the streak.

In 1930, the first ball Chicago White Sox's Pat Caraway ever pitched in the Major Leagues resulted in a triple play.

New York Yankee's Joe Glenn caught Babe Ruth's last pitching appearance in 1933.

During the 1962 All-Star Game, President John F. Kennedy told Stan Musial: "A couple years ago they told me I was too young to be president and you were too old to be playing baseball. But we fooled them."

Pitcher Bill "Looney Tunes" Faul often used self-hypnosis in order to control his pitches.

FIELDERS IN BASEBALL GAMES IN THE 1870s, WERE PROHIBITED BY A RULE CHANGE FROM CATCHING FLY BALLS WITH THEIR HATS

The first pinch-hit home run to be hit in a World Series game was knocked out of the park by the Yankee's Yogi Berri, on October 2, 1947.

Willard Brown of the St. Louis Browns was the first African-American player in the American League to hit a home run, August 13, 1947.

"Sporting goods companies pay me not to endorse their products."
– Bob Uecker

In his younger days, to prove his pitching ability, Satchell Paige stuck 4 ten-penny nails into a plank and then drove them the rest of the way in with 10 pitches from a distance of 60 feet. In 1971 Paige became the first pitcher from the Negro Leagues to be elected to the Baseball Hall of Fame.

During the 1930 season, Cleveland Indians' Joe Sewell played in 109 games and was at bat 353 times, yet struck out only 3 times.

An average Major League Baseball game uses 40 baseballs. Nearly 100,000 balls are used during the season by all 30 MLB teams. FYI -Major League baseballs are 3 inches in diameter and weigh from 5 to 5 1/4 ounces.

JAPANESE BASEBALL CATCHERS ARE TAUGHT HOW TO CROUCH BEHIND THE PLATE PROPERLY BY HAVING A **BLOCK WITH SHARP SPIKES POSITIONED BENEATH THEM.** THE GAME IS SO POPULAR THERE THAT ONE OUT OF TWO JAPANESE IS A FAN

PLAY BĒSUBŌRU!

Terry Felton of the Minnesota Twins pitched his entire big league career, 1979-1982, without a win. With a 0-16 record, he holds a Major League record for most career losses without a win.

The popular ditty, "Who Let the Dogs Out?"

by the Baha Men, was first played in a Major League stadium in June 2000 at Safeco Field, when Seattle Mariners Alex Rodriguez requested it for his batter introduction song.

Bill Voiselle, Boston Braves pitcher, wore #96 on his uniform in honor of his home town, Ninety-Six, South Carolina.

Defeated beat Difficult 5-4 in a baseball game in Defeated, Tennessee.

What a trade! Tim Fortugno, who pitched for 15 minor league teams during his career, was sold to the Milwaukee Brewers organization in 1989 for 144 baseballs, plus $2,500.

Bombs Away! Pitcher Ellis Kinder of the St. Louis Browns was on the mound on May 17, 1947 when a seagull flew over and dropped a 3-pound smelt, barely missing him. He kicked the smelt out of the way and went on for the win!

Twenty-one Major League players have hit the first pitch ever thrown to them for a home run.

Kitty Burke became the first and only woman to officially bat in a Major League game in 1935!

A fan can get much more than basic ballpark food in a baseball stadium, including sushi (Angels), Rocky Mountain Oysters (Rockies), and fish tacos (Padres)!

The League Championship games began in 1969 as a best of 5 series.

Answer from page 65

TURK WENDELL
brushed his teeth between
every inning because
he chewed _black licorice_
throughout the game!

BABE RUTH

ARRESTED FOR SPEEDING, WAS SENTENCED TO A DAY IN JAIL, BUT WAS RELEASED IN TIME TO PLAY THE LAST 3 INNINGS OF A GAME, AND GIVEN A POLICE ESCORT TO THE BALL PARK

Bob Feller of the Cleveland Indians pitched the first and only Opening Day no-hitter on April 16, 1940.

"Wee Willie" Keeler, the Baltimore Orioles' Hall of Fame right fielder explained his batting prowess simply. "Keep your eye on the ball and hit 'em where they ain't."

Babe Ruth averaged 8.5 home runs for every 100 times at bat!

While ignored by most ballpark designers, Major League Baseball Rule 1.04 states that "it is desirable" that the line from home base through the pitcher's plate to second base shall run East Northeast." If the rule is followed, the sun sets behind third base and shines on right field, where there are fewer fly balls.

> **"Any ballplayer that don't sign autographs for little kids ain't an American. He's a communist."**
> – Rogers Hornsby

Believe It or Not! In 1909, it was illegal to play baseball on a Sunday in New York City!

Every year 40,000 trees are cut to supply the bats required by America's baseball industry!

Cleveland Indians' Ray Chapman is the only modern Major League player killed by a direct hit from a pitched ball, on August 16, 1920.

Believe It or Not! The stocky Babe Ruth stole 123 bases during his career.

Ouch! Ron Hunt, playing for the Montreal Expos on September 29, 1971, became the first player to be hit by 50 pitches in one season.

Dizzy Does it Again. In the broadcast booth for the St. Louis Browns, Dizzy Dean boasted that he could still beat "9 out of 10 who call themselves pitchers," six years after he retired. Browns management saw an opportunity to boost sagging attendance and challenged Dean to prove it during the final game of the season, September 28, 1947 against the Chicago White Sox. Dean accepted and tossed 4 shutout innings and hit a single in his only time at bat!

With 35 homers in 1986, Oakland's Dave Kingman is the only Major Leaguer to hit 30-plus home runs in his last Major League season.

Believe It or Not!
AT THE BASEBALL HALL of FAME in Cooperstown, N.Y., THERE IS A BASEBALL SIGNED BY Pope John Paul II!

THE FIRST RULES OF BASEBALL MADE IT A **REQUIREMENT** THAT THE WINNING TEAM HAD TO SCORE 21 RUNS!

The Texas Rangers scored 16 of their 26 runs in the eighth inning against the Baltimore Orioles on April 19, 1996. It's the most runs ever scored during the 8th inning, which lasted 56 minutes.

Sheddan Jejeune of Evansville, Ind. threw a baseball 426 feet, 6 1/2 inches in the Central League in 1910.

Believe it or Not! A toothpick taken from Tom Seaver's game jacket that he wore from 1967 to 1969, sold at auction for $440!

The first World Series home run in Yankee Stadium was an inside-the-park homer by then New York Giant outfielder Casey Stengel, who was to go on to manage the Yankees to 10 World Series wins!

"It's a mere moment in a man's life between the All-Star Game and an old timer's game."
– Vin Scully

In 2005, the most expensive average ticket price for a Major League game is $44.56, in Boston, a 9.3% increase; the least expensive average ticket price is in Kansas City at $13.71, a 2.2% increase, according to the Team Marketing Report.

The April 11, 1907 New York Giants and Philadelphia game was forfeited after a snowball fight got out of hand.

Abner Doubleday, credited with creating the modern baseball game, fired the first gunshot from Fort Sumter while he was a captain in the Civil War in 1861.

"All managers are losers, they are the most expendable pieces of furniture on the face of the Earth."
– Ted Williams

The University of Southern California has contributed 94 players to Major League Baseball, the most of any U.S. college.

The first indoor World Series game took place in 1987 in the Minnesota Metrodome. Home field advantage and noisy crowds helped the Twin's win all four home games, and the series.

In an August 1914 game against Detroit, New York Yankees' catcher Les Nunamaker became the only Major Leaguer in the 20th century to throw out three base stealers in one inning.

"Take Me Out to the Ball Game," baseball's eternal theme song, was written in 1908 by Jack Norworth, who had never seen a professional baseball game!

Ripley Classic

JULIUS B.
SHUSTER
of Jeannette, Pa.
CAN HOLD 20 BASEBALLS
IN ONE HAND!

Rip— 7-6

93

NO SHOWS

Only one fan and none of the players showed up for the evening double header between Newark and Jersey City of the International League on July 2, 1921, and the games were called off. Everyone was more interested in the highly publicized Jack Dempsey/Georges Carpentier fight set for that evening.

Only one fan showed up for a Pacific Coast League game on October 8, 1905, between the Oakland Oaks and the Portland Beavers. According to newspaper reports, the home-plate umpire, whose job it was to announce lineups, addressed the crowd, "Dear sir..."

Official Attendance: 0. The Charleston Riverdogs set out to establish a record for the lowest attendance ever recorded. On the highly publicized "Nobody Night," in 2003, fans were not allowed into the stadium until the end of the 5th inning when the game became official. They gathered outside the stadium and listened to the game, then rushed in during the 6th inning to collect the foul balls that had landed in the empty seats.

Only one fan came to see Babe Ruth play his first game in organized baseball.

A HIGHLY ADVERTISED PROMOTIONAL GIVE-AWAY NIGHT AT COUNTY STADIUM ON JULY 29, 2000, FEATURED FREE POSTERS OF MILWAUKEE PITCHER BOB WICKMAN. UNFORTUNATELY, WICKMAN WAS TRADED TO CLEVELAND **THE NIGHT BEFORE!**

Traded for Himself! The Cleveland Indians traded catcher Harry Chiti to the New York Mets on April 25, 1962 for "a player to be named later." When the teams could not agree on another player, Chiati was returned to the Indians on June 15, 1962 as "the player to be named later."

Babe Ruth led his league in batting only once!

Among the greatest nicknames bestowed upon players in Major League history, one of the most descriptive was the one given to Hugh "Losing Pitcher" Mulcahy, a pitcher for the Phillies during the late 1930s and 1940s.

PETE ROSE

SET A NATIONAL LEAGUE RECORD IN AUGUST 1981 BY GETTING HIS 3,631 ST HIT—AND IN THE SAME MONTH, VARIATIONS OF THOSE DIGITS **WON LOTTERIES IN BOTH NEW JERSEY AND DELAWARE!**

Hall of Fame right handed pitcher Mordecai "three fingers" Brown, lost one finger and mangled two others on his right hand in a farming accident as a child, yet went on to become a respected pitcher in the Major Leagues, winning more than 200 games in 13 seasons, including 5 World Series wins.

Minor league baseball was at a peak in 1949 with 59 leagues and 448 teams. That year, 39,640,443 fans attended minor league games, a record that stood until 2004 when 39,887,755 fans showed up at minor league parks.

> **"A hot dog at the ball park is better than steak at the Ritz."**
> – Humphrey Bogart

Mandy McMichael of Florence, Italy, could put an entire baseball into her mouth!

New York Mets' Kazuo Matsui hit the first-ever pitch thrown to him over the fence in Atlanta's Turner Field in his Major League debut in 2004. He ended his rookie year with 7 homeruns, a 2.72 batting average, and $5 million richer.

That's not fair! In 1908, John McFarland of Helena of the Arkansas State League lost his perfect game when the 27th batter refused to bat, resulting in a 9-0 forfeit.

John Lubinski of Minneapolis caught his own pop fly during July 1927. He hit the ball and while running to first base fell down and as he was getting up, the ball landed in his pocket.

The Toronto Blue Jays hosted the Montreal Expos as part of the new inter-league schedule in 1997 making it the first time since WWII that the U.S. National Anthem was not heard before a Major League game.

Frank Pastore, a pitcher for the Cincinnati Reds during the 1980s once ate a 4 1/2-pound steak at the Big Texan steak ranch in Amarillo, Texas, in only 9 1/2 minutes!

THE CHICAGO CUBS

in May 1982, defeated the
Houston Astros, to become
the first American pro team
to win 8,000 games —
and believe it or not,
the winning pitcher also
scored the first run —
and his name is *RIPLEY!*

WHAT DO BABE RUTH AND W.C. FIELDS HAVE IN COMMON?

Answer on page 109

Cy Young

PITCHED FOR 22
CONSECUTIVE YEARS
IN THE MAJOR LEAGUES

He averaged more than 20
wins a season for 20 years.
He pitched 3 no-hit
no-run games!

Ripley
Classic

Rip   4-16

Japanese baseball legend Sadaharu Oh of the Tokyo Giants, hit 868 home runs during his career, 113 more than Hank Aaron!

Hoyt Wilhelm was the first relief pitcher inducted into the Baseball Hall of Fame.

Prior to becoming manager of the Brooklyn Dodgers baseball team in 1954, Walter Alston had no Major League managing experience.

Hall of Fame pitcher James "Pud" Galvin, who pitched more than 6,000 innings for several Major League teams during his 17-year career, winning 364 games, weighed in at 300-pounds!

SCORING A RUN AFTER 3 MEN ARE OUT.

BASES FULL 2 OUT. BATTER (A) WALKS FORCING RUNNER (B) HOME — BUT "B" WALKS SLOWLY TO THE PLATE. — MEANWHILE "A" IS CARELESSLY CAUGHT OFF FIRST — MAKING 3 OUTS BEFORE B SCORES AT PLATE.

Known as "Dutch" in the 1930s, U.S. President Ronald Reagan was a broadcaster for the Chicago Cubs. That's what he was doing when Hollywood "discovered" him.

Ripley Classic

THE STAR SPANGLED BANNER

WAS FIRST PLAYED PRIOR TO A BASEBALL GAME ON MAY 15, 1862 AT THE UNION GROUNDS IN BROOKLYN, N.Y., ALTHOUGH IT DIDN'T BECOME A PRE-GAME RITUAL FOR ALL GAMES — UNTIL DURING WW II.

"THE LONGEST HOME RUN"
ON April 3, 1929, BASEBALL LEGEND
LOU GEHRIG HIT A HOME RUN THAT
*TRAVELED OVER 600 FEET
from HOME PLATE!*

Team Market Report said it cost $287.84 for a
family of four to go to Fenway Park in Boston in
2007, the most expensive baseball experience of the
year. Price includes admission, parking, beverages,
food and souvenirs. The least expensive night out to a
ballpark is in Kansas City. There, it will cost a family
of four only $120.35 to attend a game. MLB average
was $171.19.

In an effort to speed up play and make the game
more interesting, the strike zone was enlarged prior to
the 1996 season. It was expanded from the top of the
knees to just below them.

Cy Williams of the Philadelphia Phillies, got a walk, a
single, a double, a triple and a home run in one game on
August 5, 1927.

In 2007, it was reported that the average salary of a Major League ball player was a record $2.92 million, while the average salary for a New York Yankee was $6.5 million. The two Florida teams, the Tampa Bay Devil Rays and the Florida Marlins were the only two teams with averages under $1 million!

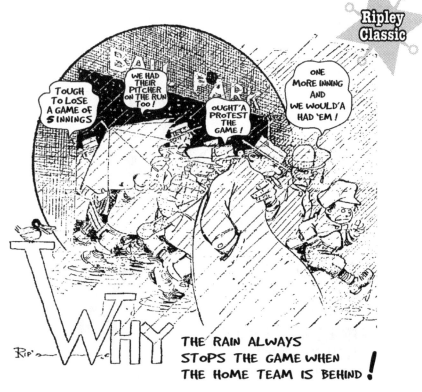

Ripley Classic

"CY" YOUNG
(ORIGINALLY CALLED "CYCLONE" BECAUSE
OF HIS TERRIFIC SPEED)

PITCHED 874 GAMES
WON 511 OF THEM
INCLUDING 3 NO-HIT-NO-RUN GAMES

A BASEBALL PLAYER
RUNNING BETWEEN
BASES -- UNTIL
ADOPTION OF MODERN
RULES IN 1845 --
**WAS PUT OUT
BY HITTING HIM
WITH THE BALL**

The June 27, 1989 game between the Baltimore Orioles and the Toronto Blue Jays was the first Major League Baseball game with opposing African-American managers – Frank Robinson versus Cito Gaston.

The first black to wear a Yankee uniform was Elston Howard. He hit a single in his first time at bat on April 14, 1955.

Baseball America lists *Bull Durham* (1988) as the best baseball motion picture of all times.

The U.S. flag rescued from the wreckage of the World Trade Center on 9/11 was flying proudly over Yankee Stadium the following month as New York City hosted the 2001 World Series.

Believe It or Not!
A LAW in Trinidad, Colo., MADE IT
ILLEGAL To PLAY **BASEBALL**
BEFORE LUNCH!

In his one and only game as a Major League pitcher, Philadelphia A's Hank Hulvey gave up a home run to Babe Ruth, the only single game pitcher to ever do so.

No Broadcasts! In 1934, fearing the loss of gate receipts, both St. Louis professional baseball teams, the Cardinals and the Browns, forbid all radio broadcasts of their home games.

The 2002 Major League All-Star game ended after 11 innings in a 7-7 tie, after both teams ran out of available pitchers.

Dmitri Young hit three home runs during the Opening Day game for the Detroit Tigers on April 4, 2005, becoming the first Tiger to do so and only the third player in Major League history to accomplish the feat.

Kansas City Athletics' Bert Campanaris performed a one-man show on September 8, 1965, setting a Major League record by playing all nine positions during one game, against the California Angels. He allowed just one run, one hit and two walks while on the mound but went 0-3 at the plate.

Olympics great Jim Thorpe had to give back the medals he won during the 1912 Olympics when it was discovered that he had earned $60 a month playing minor league baseball in 1909.

Boston Red Sox's Roger Clemens became the first pitcher in Major League history to strike out 20 hitters in one game on July 29, 1986.

Answer from page 99

BABE RUTH and W.C. FIELDS both played on the Believe It or Nots!, a charity baseball team formed in 1939 by Robert Ripley to raise money for the Boys Club Of New York City.

On June 29, 2007, BRAD TURNEY of Axexandria, La. PLAYED ALL NINE POSITIONS IN A SINGLE GAME FOR THE MINOR LEAGUE BASEBALL TEAM, THE ALEXANDRIA ACES!

Fred McGriff was the first Major League player to hit 30 home runs a season for five different teams: Blue Jays, Padres, Braves, Devil Rays and the Cubs. He's also the first and only player to hit home runs off 300 different pitchers.

Play-by-play announcer Richard Musterer called an 8 hour, 15 minute, 27-inning game in 1988 between Burlington and Bluefield, of the Appalachian League. It remains the longest continuous single-game radio broadcast in baseball history.

Phil Cavaretta is the only Major League player to be active when Babe Ruth hit his last home run in 1935 and when Hank Aaron hit his first home run in 1954.

Less than a month after signing with the New York Mets, Jimmy Piersall connected for his 100th career homer and celebrated by running the bases backward. Mets management wasn't amused and released him four days later, on June 27, 1963.

The 2001 National League champs, the Arizona Diamondbacks, was the youngest franchise in Major League history to make it to the World Series.

Dick Stuart, nicknamed Dr. Strangeglove for his unpredictable fielding ability, led the league in errors by a first baseman for 7 consecutive years, 1958-1964.

Baseball is the only professional sport in which the coaches wear the same uniform as the players.

Catcher Hank Gowdy of the New York Giants tripped over his own catcher's mask as he ran for a foul ball pop-up from Muddy Ruel during the 1924 World Series, and missed the ball. Ruel then doubled and later that inning scored the winning run, giving Washington its first-ever World Series championship.

In 1989, Texas Rangers' Nolan Ryan struck out 301 batters, the most ever for a 40-year old.

A Big Couch Was Needed! After losing 95 games in 1947, 94 games in 1948 and 101 in 1949, The St. Louis Browns hired David F. Tracy, a New York psychologist & hypnotist, to help the team overcome its loser's complex. The team dumped Tracy in May 1950 when the Browns started off the season with an 8 – 25 record.

A game inside the behemoth Astrodome was rained out! Following a deluge that dropped nearly 10 inches of rain, streets throughout the city were under as much as four feet of water. Nobody could get to the dome! Only 30 fans made it to the June 15, 1976 game, between the Houston Astros and the Pittsburgh Pirates before it was called!

Baseball heaven? Babe Ruth and Billy Martin are both buried in the Gate of Heaven Cemetery in Hawthorne, New York, 25 miles north of Yankee Stadium!

Ripley Classic

THE
BABE

The Classic Baseball • • • • • • • • • •
• • • • • • • • • • • • in Heaven Story

Two 90-year old men, Moe and Sam, have been friends all their lives. Sam is dying of cancer, and Moe comes to visit him every day.

"Sam," says Moe. "You know how we have both loved baseball all our lives, and how we played minor league ball together for so many years. Sam, you have to do me one favor. When you get to heaven, somehow you've got to let me know if there's baseball up there."

Sam looks up at Moe from his death bed. "Moe, you've been my best friend many years. This favor, if it is at all possible, I'll do for you."

Sam passed on shortly after that conversation. At midnight several nights after Sam died, Moe was awakened by a blinding flash of light. A voice calls out to him, "Moe, Moe."

"Who is it?" says Moe sitting up. "Who is it?"

"Moe, it's me, Sam."

Moe answers. "Come on. You're not Sam. Sam just died."

"I'm telling you," insists the voice. "It's me, Sam!"

"Where are you?" questioned Moe.

"I'm in heaven," says Sam. " I've got really good news and a little bad news."

"So, tell me the good news first," says Moe.

"The good news," says Sam, "is that there is baseball in heaven. All our buddies who've gone before us are here. Better yet, we're all young men again. And even better, it's always springtime and it never rains or snows. And best of all, we can play baseball all we want. We never get tired!"

"Really?" says Moe. "That is fantastic, wonderful, beyond my wildest dreams! But, what's the bad news?"

"You're pitching next Tuesday."

115

Acknowledgements ·

In addition to reading (and totally enjoying) more than 2,000 baseball Believe It or Not! entries currently housed in the Ripley archives, I spent countless hours researching for new, weird and unbelievable facts. I found some great stuff, but I had enormous help along the way.

In 2005, a version of this book was sent out to more than 500 baseball writers and broadcasters throughout the United States as a quirky media guide. They loved it and I received many responses with additional Believe It or Not! ideas about the teams they cover, as well as encouragement to expand and update the book and make it available to baseball fans throughout the world. Thanks to all who responded.

Also many thanks go out to members of the Society of American Baseball Researchers (SABR) for their assistance. Edward Meyer, VP Archives & Exhibits for Ripley Entertainment was a great assistance in helping me dig up all the Ripley Classics.

Special kudos go out to my new friend, author Dan Schlossberg who has written 32 books on baseball and thousands of articles on the sport. He encouraged me, helped point my research in the right direction, and even used several of our Ripley's Believe It or Not! cartoons in his new book, *Baseball Gold*.

Thanks to all, you are now part of Ripley history! Believe It or Not!

Tim O'Brien, Author

About Us •

Ripley Entertainment (www.ripleys.com) is a
leading global entertainment company with
more than 60 attractions in 10 countries, and
an annual attendance of more than 13 million
visitors. In addition to its world-class aquariums
in Myrtle Beach, S.C. and Gatlinburg, Tenn.,
the company owns and operates Ripley's Believe
it or Not! museums, Ripley's Moving Theaters,
Louis Tussaud's Wax Museums, Guinness
World Records Attractions, Ripley's Haunted
Adventures, and Ripley's Davy Crockett Mini-
Golf and Old MacDonald's Farm Mini-Golf
courses. In 2006, the company entered the
hospitality industry when it built the 406-room
Great Wolf Lodge indoor waterpark resort
in Niagara Falls, Canada. The Orlando-based
company has successful publishing and broadcast
divisions that oversee projects including the
globally syndicated Believe It or Not! television
show, best selling Believe It or Not! books and
the popular syndicated Believe It or Not! comic
strip, still seen in nearly 200 newspapers in 42
countries. Ripley Entertainment is a division
of the Jim Pattison Group, the third largest
privately owned company in Canada.

John Graziano *(ILLUSTRATOR, PICTURED AS CATCHER)*
is only the fifth person to take up the pen as the
official illustrator for Ripley`s Believe It or Not! Prior
to joining the Ripley team in 2004, and following
his education at the Newark School of Fine and
Industrial Arts and the Art Institute of Pittsburgh,
John designed trading card sets and a portrait series
based on the 1960s cult TV show "Dark Shadows."
He has also created comic strips for "Scream Queens"
magazine, sculpted figures that have been made into
wax museum pieces, provided book illustrations,
designed t-shirt graphics and created storyboards
and concept drawings for Hollywood films. John is
a bass player and vocalist in a 1960s tribute band
appropriately called "60`s Groove."

Tim O'Brien *(AUTHOR, PICTURED AT BAT)*, VP Publishing
& Communications for Ripley Entertainment Inc.
is responsible for coordinating the publicity and
promotion of the company's 65-plus attractions
throughout the world and serves as the company's
national spokesman. Prior to his position with Ripley,
Tim served 18 years as senior editor of *Amusement
Business,* the world's leading business magazine for the
amusement park and attraction industries. During his
colorful career, the award winning photojournalist has
had nearly 10,000 articles and 5,000 photos published
and has written 12 books. His previous three books
published by Ripley Publishing were *Ripley's Believe It
or Not! Amusement Park Oddities and Trivia, The Wave
Maker – The Story of Theme Park Pioneer George Millay,*
and *Legends – Pioneers of the Amusement Park Industry.*

CPSIA information can be obtained
at www.ICGtesting.com
Printed in the USA
LVHW050829020919
629647LV00013B/610